SPIRITUAL BLESSINGS IN CHRIST

by susan sherwood parr

Published by

WORD PRODUCTIONS

PO BOX 11865, ALBUQUERQUE, NM 87192 USA

WORDPRODUCTIONS.ORG

Spiritual Blessings In Christ
by Susan Sherwood Parr

Copyright ©2015 by Susan Sherwood Parr
http://www.susanparr.org
http://www.lifetotheworldministries.org

Published by Word Productions LLC
PO Box 11865
Albuquerque, NM 87192

Printed in the United States of America.

ISBN 978-0-9909245-8-6

Table of Contents

Spiritual Blessings

BLESSED BE THE GOD AND FATHER OF OUR LORD
JESUS CHRIST, WHO HAS BLESSED US WITH EVERY
SPIRITUAL BLESSING IN THE HEAVENLY PLACES IN
CHRIST. EPHESIANS 1:3

In Ephesians 1:3, the Scripture says, "He HAS (past tense) blessed us with every spiritual blessing in heavenly places in Christ." When the Apostle Paul wrote a letter to the church, he was talking to all believers in Jesus Christ. We can be confident in knowing that what is given for one, because he or she is a Christian, is given to us all. So then, there are spiritual blessings given to us by the Holy Spirit when we are born again through the

1

blood of Jesus Christ and become part of His family. Although God's ways of blessing His people are limitless, and although He is not limited to spiritual blessings, we will be studying the "spiritual blessings" of Ephesians 1:3.

When you first read that Scripture, you can only receive a mild understanding of what the Holy Spirit is trying to get across to the Body of Christ. But, if you will begin to meditate on it, the depth and richness contained in its meaning will open up to you.

One day, while I was having devotions, I was seeking the Lord in His Word. I love the book of Ephesians! It teaches a lot about what happens to a person who becomes a Christian. So, as I sat on the couch, I started to try to meditate on the Scriptures. I got down to Ephesians 1:3: "...Who has blessed us with every spiritual blessing." HAS blessed us? What on earth did God mean?

As I began to meditate on the verse and to pray, I realized some of the great spiritual blessings we possess as Christians. Soon, with pen in hand, I began to write. What would happen if I meditated on all of the Scriptures like that? I didn't expect the revelation. The words I was writing made simple, clear sense.

We Have Spiritual Blessings!

We have spiritual blessings! That is an amazing and wonderful fact. It's exciting to think about it. What are they? How can we find out what Paul is trying to convey? As you read this, please understand that I am not saying that these blessings are a "new doctrine." I will simply share with you those I believe the Holy Spirit has allowed me to see for the purpose of inspiring your love for the Lord, His Word, and for the beauty of His grace.

We will take the spiritual blessings individually, so that we can study what Jesus has done for us and what now belongs to each of us because of the complete redemptive work of the Cross of Christ.

The New Birth

BLESSED BE THE GOD AND FATHER OF OUR LORD
JESUS CHRIST, WHO HAS BLESSED US WITH EVERY
SPIRITUAL BLESSING IN THE HEAVENLY PLACES IN
CHRIST. EPHESIANS 1:3

The NEW BIRTH, which is really our
spiritual birth into Christ, is the most
vital and important of the spiritual blessings in Christ. It is the first and necessary step to take in order to be able to
receive the other spiritual blessings in
Christ.

By asking Jesus Christ to forgive us of
our sins, to come into our hearts, and to
be the Lord of our lives, we can be born
again. What does that mean?

"Born again" is *not* a trite phrase that turns people off when they hear it. What did Jesus mean when He said those words? Let's look at the biblical account:

There was a man of the Pharisees named Nicodemus, a ruler of the Jews. This man came to Jesus by night and said to Him, "Rabbi, we know that You are a teacher come from God; for no one can do these signs that You do unless God is with him." Jesus answered and said to him, "Most assuredly, I say to you, unless one is born again, he cannot see the kingdom of God." Nicodemus said to Him, "How can a man be born when he is old? Can he enter a second time into his mother's womb and be born?" Jesus answered, "Most assuredly, I say to you, unless one is born of water and the Spirit, he cannot enter the kingdom of God. That which is born of the flesh is flesh, and that which is born of the Spirit is spirit. Do not marvel that I said to you, 'You must be born again.' The wind blows where it wishes,

and you hear the sound of it, but cannot tell where it comes from and where it goes. So is everyone who is born of the Spirit."
Nicodemus answered and said to Him, "How can these things be?"
Jesus answered and said to him, "Are you the teacher of Israel, and do not know these things? Most assuredly, I say to you, We speak what We know and testify what We have seen, and you do not receive Our witness. If I have told you earthly things and you do not believe, how will you believe if I tell you heavenly things? No one has ascended to heaven but He who came down from heaven, that is, the Son of Man who is in heaven. And as Moses lifted up the serpent in the wilderness, even so must the Son of Man be lifted up, that whoever believes in Him should not perish but have eternal life. For God so loved the world that He gave His only begotten Son, that whoever believes in Him should not perish but have

everlasting life. For God did not send His Son into the world to condemn the world, but that the world through Him might be saved. He who believes in Him is not condemned; but he who does not believe is condemned already, because he has not believed in the name of the only begotten Son of God. John 3:1-18

What Did Jesus Mean: "Born Again"?

In this Scripture, Jesus told Nicodemus that he *must* be born again. Those words sound strange to someone who has never heard this expressed. If we can understand what this means, we will better be able to share the gospel with others. Remember to choose your words when sharing your Christian faith with others. Too frequently, when we become Christians, we start speaking Christianese. We say things like, "You need to be born again" or "repent." We can sound ridiculous. Why don't we speak in conversational words and in words easily understood? Let's learn a lesson: We can translate God's Word into street language. Think about what Jesus meant, as we take a look at several scriptures. The Holy Spirit can enlighten your understanding.

In 2 Corinthians 5:17 we read about what Jesus was trying to describe to Nicodemus: "Therefore if any man be in Christ, he is a new creature: old things are passed away; behold, all things are become new."

Paul was teaching believers that when they became followers of Christ, a transformation would take place.

When you look up the Greek translation for "creation" in *Vine's Expository Dictionary of New Testament Words*, you will find that it means the following:

> **Creation as a noun, 2937, ktisis:**
> Primarily "the act of creating," or "the creative act in process," as in 2 Corinthians 5:17 "new creation": As to its use in Gal. 6:15; 2 Cor. 5:17, in the former, apparently, "the reference is to the creative act of God, whereby a man is introduced into the blessing of salvation, in contrast to circumcision done by human hands, which the

*Judaizers claimed was necessary
to that end. In 2 Cor. 5:17 the ref-
erence is to what the believer is in
Christ; in consequence of the
creative act he has become a new
creature."* (*From Notes on
Galatians, by Hogg and Vine, p. 339.)*

If any man is in Christ he is a new
creation. Something supernatural really
does take place. If you haven't experienced it, you can. You will be created,
built by the Holy Spirit. The sacrifice of
Christ is enough for you to become
"born again."

Something Was Missing

I remember, after years of being a
dedicated, denominational Christian,
praying to ask Jesus into my heart. The
whole thing had sounded strange to me.
I had never heard people talk like that.

When I lived in Georgia, a woman
once came to my home to invite me to
her church. While there in my small living
room, she suddenly began to gasp and
huff and preach. It was so strange. That
is not the way to win someone to Christ.

10

She thought she was under the power of the Holy Spirit. I know this now, after becoming a Christian. Why did she do that, when she sounded so foolish? People like that will argue that "...the Gospel is foolishness..and the power of God to Salvation." But that is NOT what is meant by the following verses:

> *For I am not ashamed of the gospel of Christ, for it is the power of God to salvation for everyone who believes, for the Jew first and also for the Greek.* Romans 1:1

> *For the message of the cross is foolishness to those who are perishing, but to us who are being saved it is the power of God.*
> 1 Corinthians 1:18

God is talking about how Jesus coming to die for our sins, doesn't make sense to the world. He is not saying to present the Gospel in a foolish manner. Do you see the difference?

The woman didn't know it, but I was already praying and dedicating every day to God. I believed Jesus died for the sins of the world and for mine. Even so, there was something missing. It is better that we not assume anything when we speak to people about Christ. There are some wonderful and creative ways to share what God means to us.

Good Advice

The best teaching I ever heard about witnessing to someone was through a Campus Crusade for Christ Bible study. The Bible teacher explained to us that we should pray something like this:

> *Lord, I don't know what this person needs to hear or what I should say. I give my vocal chords and lips to you. I yield myself to You, speak in and through me, in Jesus' name.*

Every time I prayed that prayer I received great results. Perhaps it was because the woman in Georgia spoke to me in the unique way she did; as I was always sensitive to talking to people at their own level and in their own manner of speaking.

Thank God, someone explained to me that "into my heart" meant into my spirit, the depths of my being. That made sense. I wish I had heard it explained that way to me when I was a child. Why hadn't anyone said it just like that? Why didn't they tell me that it was the Holy Spirit coming into my spirit? Speak in English, or in whatever tongue the person needs to hear the message.

How I Prayed

I prayed the prayer to ask Jesus to come into my heart and life a couple of years later. But when I prayed I said, "Lord, if you can do that (come into someone's heart/spirit), and if there is anything I don't have, I want it." What happened amazed me. For the first time in my life, I felt love on the inside of me. A couple of people around me asked, "What has happened to you? You look different." The prayer and corresponding experience had even changed my appearance. I really was brand new. Then, as I began to stay in church, attend Bible studies, and read the Bible, I could actually feel myself changing. It was incredible. I had been born again.

What Happens?

Through the "new birth" we are enabled by the Holy Spirit, to come into a relationship with our heavenly Father and with His Son, Jesus Christ. Through this new birth, we are made partakers of His love and grace and are now a part of God's family. Receiving the new birth and leading others to this experience is something we want to do as Christians. I have had a some opportunities to lead people to Christ. I believe it is one of the greatest gifts we can give to another. Here is one such experience.

The Man on the Street

While working in downtown Tulsa, Oklahoma, I kept passing a certain man on the street while finding a parking space, and even during my lunch hour. He was shabbily dressed, and it was a disturbing experience just to pass him there. He was dirty and he had an empty and unhappy look on his face. Every time I passed him by, the thought came to me: "Why don't you tell him about Jesus?" Every direction I went, there he was. I began to get the message. I told God that if I saw him again I would speak

14

to him. I was torn between wondering what people would think if I was speaking to a man that looked like he did, and the knowledge of what could happen to his life if he would invite Jesus into his heart. I told him that he could have the life-changing power of God move in his life.

That morning, I was running a little late for work. I parked the car farther away than usual, got out of my car, and began to walk up the street. There was that same man again. I walked across the street and began to tell him about the love of God, and of how God wanted people to be blessed and happy. I told him that there was nothing too hard for God; that there was no life, no condition, and no set of circumstances too hard for God to heal or to change. I told of God's miracle power in my own life, and of the POWER OF GOD working inside of me and changing me. I began to telling him about a difficult time I once went through.

Tell What Is Vital

When leading someone into salvation, do not share things that aren't going to help them. If you pray before you talk and consider this fact, you will do well.

I spoke to him from the heart about Jesus and he was moved, really moved. God will allow the power of the Holy Spirit to flow through you as you share your story with others.

"God can give you what you don't have," I said. "God never intended a man to change himself; the Holy Spirit does the work. God can heal your life, and anyone else's, no matter what their case might be. He can help you get a job." I saw a little light in the man's eyes.

I asked him if I could pray for him and he said "yes." First, I prayed for God to bless his life. The door was wide open. He was moved inside and there on the street he asked Jesus into his heart. I didn't just leave him there. I gave him a small booklet for new believers and gave him the phone number to the church I was attending. There he could get counseling, meet people who would pray with him, and get some decent clothes to wear.

16

I had obeyed God, and this man had heard the GOOD NEWS.

Spiritual Blessing One

ALL THINGS ARE MADE NEW and OF GOD by the Spirit of God. Jesus forgives our sins when we ask Him; the Holy Spirit comes into our hearts; and God's Holy Spirit begins His work in us. Spiritual life has come to us through Christ. We are united to our heavenly Father in a supernatural way. If you have accepted that Jesus Christ died for your sins, rose again from the dead, and is seated at the right hand of the Father; you have asked Him to forgive you of your sins and to come into your heart and take control of your life, you too, have a new life in Christ. This is the first spiritual blessing in Jesus Christ.

The Scriptural Proof

Therefore, if anyone is in Christ, he is a new creation, old things have passed away, behold, all things have become new. Now all things are of God, who has reconciled us to

Himself through Jesus Christ, and given us the ministry of reconciliation. 2 Corinthians 5:17–18

Therefore, just as through one man sin, and thus death spread to all men, because all sinned.
Romans 5:12

For if by the one man's offense death reigned through the one, much more those who receive abundance of grace and of the gift of righteousness will reign in life through the One, Jesus Christ.
Romans 5:17

Having been born again, not of corruptible seed but incorruptible, through the Word of God which lives and abides forever.
1 Peter 1:23

CHAPTER THREE

Partakers of His Divine Nature

BLESSED BE THE GOD AND FATHER OF OUR LORD
JESUS CHRIST, WHO HAS BLESSED US WITH EVERY
SPIRITUAL BLESSING IN THE HEAVENLY PLACES IN
CHRIST. EPHESIANS 1:3

Did you know the Bible teaches that all provisions or promises in God's Word belong to you? It's true: "Then Peter opened his mouth, and said, Of a truth I perceive that God is no respecter of persons:" (Acts 10:34). What He has given to Christians in the Bible, He has given to all Christians.

There is a Scripture that says that we are partakers of His divine nature. Well, we already know that He has come to live within us in the person of the Holy Spirit. The Holy Spirit IS His divine nature. He IS God. Think about that! But it is true. This is the second spiritual blessing in Christ. Here is the Bible verse:

...As His divine power has given to us all things that pertain to life and godliness, through the knowledge of Him who called us by glory and virtue; By which have been given to us exceeding great and precious promises; that through these you may be partakers of the divine nature, having escaped the corruption that is in the world through lust. 2 Peter 1:3-4

The man on the street in downtown Tulsa, Oklahoma, became a partaker of the divine nature of God. The blood of Jesus Christ washed him of his sins, and from the moment he prayed, the Holy Spirit began to dwell on the inside of him.

We are partakers of the His divine nature, and, as Christians, we have been given ALL THINGS that pertain to LIFE and GODLINESS (2 Peter 1:3). Did you get that? *All things* that pertain to life and all things that have to do with godliness. God promises this. We should meditate on it until it sinks in.

First, the Spiritual

Although all of these blessings in Christ can be related to the natural side of your life because they affect the natural part of your life also, for the purpose of this study, I want you to first consider the spiritual. After all, the blessings first take place in the spiritual realm. Every good thing we possess because we are Christians has been given to us because of the redemptive work of Jesus Christ. It is because He died for our sins that we can now come into the kingdom of God. So, think of the spiritual first. First, we receive a spiritual blessing of the Holy Spirit in our lives. Next, it will be obvious to those around me because my life has changed. Here's one of my favorite verses that depicts His divine nature affecting our lives:

> *For this reason we also thank God without ceasing, because when you received the word of God which*

*you heard from us, you welcomed
it not as the word of men, but as it
is in truth, the word of God, which
also effectually works in you who
believe.* 1 Thessalonians 2:13

God Living In You and Me?

Think about God living inside of us,
about His love and His kindness, etc.
God changes us. He causes it to happen
to us. We can't do it ourselves. Thank
God, He can change us! Look at these
Old Testament scriptures promising that
God will change us:

*"I will put My Spirit within you and
cause you to walk in My statutes,
and you will keep My judgments
and do them."* Ezekiel 36:27

*For it is God who works in you
both to will and to do for His good
pleasure.* Philippians 2:13

What a marvelous thought: Not only
will the Lord live within us, but He's going
to help us to do as He desires.

CHAPTER FOUR

Access to the Grace of God

BLESSED BE THE GOD AND FATHER OF OUR LORD
JESUS CHRIST, WHO HAS BLESSED US WITH EVERY
SPIRITUAL BLESSING IN THE HEAVENLY PLACES IN
CHRIST. EPHESIANS 1:3

What does the "grace of God" mean?
"Grace," when looked at in the
Greek language can be interpreted *love
gifts* or *unmerited favor from God.* I
would describe it as this:

> *The grace of God is a gift of the
> love of God to enable us to be
> what we need to be; His compas-
> sion and power being poured out
> on us to meet every need or cir-
> cumstance according to His will.*

23

Baker's Evangelical Dictionary of Biblical Theology defines grace:

> *The word "grace" in biblical parlance can, like forgiveness, repentance, regeneration, and salvation, mean something as broad as describing the whole of God's activity toward man or as narrow as describing one segment of that activity. An accurate, common definition describes grace as the unmerited favor of God toward man. In the Old Testament, the term that most often is translated "grace," is hen (ej); in the New Testament, it is charis (cavri).*

Manifold Grace

Grace is the third spiritual blessing in our study. Let's look at the manifold grace of God. Sometimes grace is unseen and is grace in our hearts or in circumstances that are developing; at other times, it is seen in great miracles. Here is a story that displays God's grace in action.

24

Some time ago, my eldest son had been playing outside his grandmother's house. He was running and playing in her yard. He wasn't expecting it at all when he stumbled over a yellow jacket's nest in a hole in the ground. He was badly stung and suffered an allergic reaction. Immediately, he was taken to the emergency room of the hospital in the little town where we lived.

As soon as I was informed of what had happened, I began to pray and to remind the Lord of the promises in His Word. I had no idea that he experienced an allergic reaction.

I arrived at the hospital, rushed to the emergency room, and opened the door. There, on the emergency room table, lay my convulsing son with a pale bluish color to his body. The doctor was working with him. I walked in the door, gasped, and said, "Jesus, mercy!"

I said it spontaneously, not even realizing what I was saying. Instantly, Roy stopped convulsing! They took my son to a room.

The doctor came in the room and said, "That little prayer worked!" What

power and grace there is in God! His power,
love, and compassion are without measure!
He is such a kind and loving God.

Grace In Action

I watched the grace of God in motion.
The power of the Holy Spirit raised my
son up. It is exciting to see the grace
and power of God and His Word in
action. It works.

When you need help in your life and
the answer doesn't seem to come
through "Jesus, Mercy," realize that it
only seems like the answer isn't coming.
Have faith in God. Believe me, He hears
you, He cares, and He is answering your
cries. God's grace is available to you.

It's Not Just "Say It and Get it"

Some time ago, a minister prayed for
me. I asked him why I couldn't seem to
get the answer. His reply to me was "just
keep saying it." While he was sincere,
he was sincerely wrong. It is good to say
you are trusting God, but there are those
who have misinterpreted God's Word
and taught others to turn God into their
servant and a puppet by making a magic

wand out of how many times you say a scripture. This is false teaching.

How Can I Walk In Faith?

How can you walk in faith? Here are four steps that will help you:

1. Pray to the Father in Jesus' name, as He teaches us in His Word.

2. Let your specific and scriptural requests be made known to God (Philippians 6:7-8).

3. Thank God for what He is doing according to His will. You will find that many things are God's will.

4. When you are finished praying and rest the whole of your personality on Who God is, His integrity and the integrity of His Word, and on His promises in His Word, your prayers are always answered. He may not always do what you ask, but He can lead you to pray in a different way. Stay close to the Lord. Put God and His Word first in your life. You will be amazed at the specific answers to prayer that you receive.

I am part of the prayer group that prays during the services at the church I attend. We pray specifically, trust in God's Word, praise and thank Him for His answers...and we are literally amazed at the glorious answers.

Scriptures Promising Grace

The spiritual blessing of access to the grace of God is confirmed in the following scriptures:

Therefore, having been justified by faith, we have peace with God through our Lord Jesus Christ, through whom also we have access by faith into this grace in which we stand, and rejoice in hope of the glory of God. Romans 5:1–2

For if by one man's offense death reigned through the one, much more, those who receive abundance of grace and of the gift of righteousness will reign in life by one, Jesus Christ. Romans 5:17

And of His fullness we have all received, and grace for grace. For the law was given through Moses,

*but grace and truth came through
Jesus Christ.* John 1:16–17

The spiritual blessing of this grace existing in our lives is confirmed through the following scriptures:

*When he came and had seen the
grace of God, he was glad, and
encouraged them all that with purpose of heart they should continue
with the Lord.* Acts 11:23

*Therefore they stayed there a long
time, speaking boldly in the Lord,
who was bearing witness to the
word of His grace, granting signs
and wonders to be done by their
hands.* Acts 14:3

*From there they sailed to Antioch,
where they had been commended
to the grace of God for the work
which they had completed.*
Acts 14:26

*So now, brethren, I commend you
to God and to the word of His
grace, which is able to build you up
and give you an inheritance among
all those who are sanctified.*
Acts 20:32

CHAPTER FIVE

Forgiveness of Sins

BLESSED BE THE GOD AND FATHER OF OUR LORD
JESUS CHRIST, WHO HAS BLESSED US WITH EVERY
SPIRITUAL BLESSING IN THE HEAVENLY PLACES IN
CHRIST. EPHESIANS 1:3

D id you know that God can forgive
your sins? Do you know what it does
to you to be cleansed? Modern medical
science and psychology have discovered
that people get well when they forgive
and let grudges go, and when they know
they are forgiven. The forgiveness of sins
is the next spiritual blessing in the study.

Here are some scriptures mentioning
forgiveness:

*If we confess our sins, He is faith-
ful and just to forgive us our sins
and to cleanse us from all unright-
eousness.* 1 John 1:9

*In Him we have redemption (the
finished complete, more-than-
enough work of the cross of Jesus
Christ) through His blood, the forgiveness of sins, according to the
riches of His grace.* Ephesians 1:7

Medical Science and Forgiveness

Below is an excerpt from an issue of
Stanford Medicine, Volume 16 Number 4,
SUMMER 1999, which is published quar-
terly by Stanford University Medical
Center, aims to keep readers informed
about the education, research, clinical
care and other goings-on at the medical
center:

The Art and Science
of Forgiveness

*If you feel good but want to feel even
better, try forgiving someone.*
                    —FREDERIC LUSKIN, PHD

*For centuries, the world's religious
and spiritual traditions have recom-*

mended the use of forgiveness as a balm for hurt or angry feelings. Psychotherapists have worked to help their clients forgive, and some have written about the importance of forgiveness. Until recently, however, the scientific literature has not had much to say about the effect of forgiveness. But that's starting to change. While the scientific study of forgiveness is just beginning—the relevant intervention research having been conducted only during the past ten years—when taken together, the work so far demonstrates the power of forgiveness to heal emotional wounds and hints that forgiveness may play a role in physical healing as well.

What is intriguing about this research is that even people who are not depressed or particularly anxious can obtain the improved emotional and psychological functioning that comes from learning to forgive. This suggests that forgiveness may enable *people who are functioning adequately to feel even better. Published studies on forgiveness have shown the importance of forgiveness training on coping with a variety of psychologically painful experiences. Studies have been conducted with adolescents who felt neglected by their parents, with women who were abused as children, with elderly women who felt hurt or uncared for, with males who disagreed with their female partners' decisions to have abortions and with college students who had been hurt. These studies showed that when given forgiveness training of varying lengths and intensities, participants could become less hurt and become more able to forgive their offenders.*

Receiving Forgiveness

Forgiving others is very powerful. Receiving forgiveness is even more powerful. Think about having a clear conscience and the peace of mind. God gives this to us. Forgive, and be forgiven.

We Are Redeemed

Jesus paid the price for our redemption. He bought us back from the hands of Satan with the priceless sacrifice of His life's blood. It was more than enough. Jesus accomplished the work, defeating satan once and for all:

Having disarmed principalities and powers, He made a public spectacle of them, triumphing over them (the principalities and powers of darkness) in it. Colossians 2:15

He has delivered us from the power of darkness and conveyed us into the kingdom of the Son of His love. Colossians 1:13

Miracle for a Hard Heart

I heard a story about a man on death row. His mother had prayed for him for many, many years. He was a murderer. His heart was filled with hatred, and he refused to listen to anyone talk about Jesus. The story went something like this:

One day, in his cell on death row, and while in the deepest despair, the Holy Spirit gave him a vision: he saw Jesus Christ on the Cross. He saw the beaten, bleeding body of Jesus, and eyes full of compassion and love looking right at him.

God touched that man's heart. Instantly LOVE began pouring into that criminal's heart. The hatred was drained from his heart by the power of the love of God. He had received Jesus.

This was the beginning of miracles for this man's life. He had been transferred into the kingdom of the Son of God. The blood of Christ had cleansed him from all sin.

The cleansing power of the blood of Christ is ours. As Christians, we miss it once in a while, and when we do, the Bible says He is faithful and just to forgive us and cleanse us. What a promise!

In whom we have redemption through His blood...even the forgiveness of sins! Colossians 1:14

But there is forgiveness with You, that You may be feared. Psalm 130:4

Jesus Understands You

If anyone understands your problems and shortcomings, it's God. With His compassion, love, and grace He reaches out and forgives us of our sins. Forgiveness is yours and it's mine. Just ask Him. No matter what the evil is or may have been in your life, the blood of Jesus Christ and its cleansing power is greater.

For God so loved the world that He gave His only begotten Son, that whoever believes in Him should not perish but have everlasting life.
John 3:16

C H A P T E R   S I X

Baptism of the Holy Spirit

BLESSED BE THE GOD AND FATHER OF OUR LORD
JESUS CHRIST, WHO HAS BLESSED US WITH EVERY
SPIRITUAL BLESSING IN THE HEAVENLY PLACES IN
CHRIST. EPHESIANS 1:3

Have you heard of the baptism of the
Holy Spirit? What an awesome con-
cept. The Word teaches us that it exists
and that we can have it. This is our next
spiritual blessing. Baptism is an immers-
ing. Immersion in the Holy Spirit? Is that
possible?

After a person accepts Jesus Christ as
the Lord and Savior of his or her life,
they are indeed a NEW CREATION (2
Corinthians 5:17). Spiritual death has

been eradicated and the recipient
receives life through the Spirit; the
Holy Spirit has come to dwell within
that person.

When Was the New Birth Possible?

Before Jesus died on the cross, and
before the redemptive work was finished,
it was impossible for anyone to experience the new birth (salvation). So then,
after Jesus died and rose from the dead
and went to be seated at the right hand
of the Father, Jesus' disciples became
born again or new creations in Christ.
The exact time is not stated; however,
after the redemptive work of Calvary was
complete, it became possible for the
entire human race to be born again.

Something More

Even though the new birth is the
greatest miracle that can happen to a
person, Jesus Himself said that there was
something more. Here is a scriptural
account of these born-again believers
being told about the baptism of the Holy
Spirit:

The former account I made, O

*Theophilus, of all that Jesus began
both to do and teach, until the day
in which He was taken up, after He
through the Holy Spirit had given
commandments to the apostles
whom He had chosen, to whom He
also presented Himself alive after
His suffering by many infallible
proofs, being seen by them during
forty days and speaking of the
things pertaining to the kingdom of
God. And being assembled together with them, He commanded
them not to depart from
Jerusalem, but to wait for the
Promise of the Father, "which," He
said, "you have heard from Me; for
John truly baptized with water, but
you shall be baptized with the Holy
Spirit not many days from now."*
Acts 1:1-5

What Does the Bible Say?

Think about this for a moment: Jesus'
followers were already "Christians." As
soon as the redemptive work of the
Cross was accomplished, they were able
to be born again because the penalty for

sin had been paid. This means that as Christians, the Holy Spirit already was dwelling in them. We know that. This is taught in churches around the world: When we accept Christ, the Holy Spirit immediately comes to live within us. Followers of Christ, those in whom the Holy Spirit dwelled, were told to assemble and "wait for the promise of the Father," which Jesus had told them about. Jesus said, "Which you have heard from Me." When did Jesus tell them about this? Here is the Scripture:

"Behold, I send the Promise of My Father upon you; but tarry in the city of Jerusalem until you are endued with power from on high."
Luke 24:49

The Day of Pentecost

In Acts 1 is the record of Christians receiving the baptism in the Holy Spirit. Here is another Scripture describing an outpouring of the Holy Spirit. It is the verse Peter used to explain what was happening to them:

"And it shall come to pass in the last days," says God, *"that I will pour out*

My spirit on all flesh; your sons and
your daughters shall prophesy, your
young men shall see visions, your old
men shall dream dreams." Acts 2:17

When the Holy Ghost had come, Peter
was empowered by the Holy Spirit to
explain to the people what was happening. They preached the Gospel, they
prophesied, and they began to speak with
other tongues as the Holy Spirit gave them
utterance.

Not Received with Water Baptism?
The Baptism of the Holy Spirit and the
baptism with water are two different experiences or events:

Who, when they had come down,
prayed for them that they might
receive the Holy Spirit. For as yet He
had fallen upon none of them. They
had only been baptized in the name
of the Lord Jesus. Then they laid
hands on them, and they received
the Holy Spirit. Acts 8:15-17

My Baptism in the Holy Spirit
After I had been born again, I began
to really dig into the Word of God. The

desire to be closer to God was growing
within me. I had been learning how to be
led by the Holy Spirit, and God was
becoming a more manifested reality in
my life, when suddenly things changed,
and I found myself in an onslaught of
temptation I had never before experienced. It seemed like the power over
my circumstances in life wasn't found
within me. It really scared me. I didn't
want to fall.

One day, as I was driving down the
road, I prayed, "God, isn't there something more? I just won't make it if this is
all there is."

I Needed Something More

I needed more power in my life. It
began there. Soon after I prayed, I shared
this with my friend Donna. She told me
about some interdenominational prayer
meetings she and her husband had been
attending and invited me.

Donna tried to prepare me. "The
prayer meeting is in a psychologist's base-
ment. Kids from ages sixteen to twenty-
four were there." Finally, I decided to go.

After arriving, the leader had us all sit
in a circle on the floor. He led us into

prayer, telling us to just spend a little time thanking God.

Around the room people were saying, "Thank you, Jesus. Thank you, Jesus. I love you, Jesus."

I thought, "Okay, I can whisper 'thank you, Jesus...I love you, Jesus.'"

The leader began again, "Lord, you promise that when two or more are gathered in Your name, You are there in the midst of them. I claim this promise." After he prayed, for the first time in my life, I felt the manifest presence of God. As they praised God the room was filled with what felt like a liquid love.

The Jesus Movement

This was during the Jesus Movement in the 60s and 70s. Miracles were happening all over. When people at churches or in concerts got up to sing, the presence of God filled the place where they were ministering. The Jesus Movement was a special outpouring of the Holy Spirit. At the end of the meeting, the psychologist asked if anyone there wanted to receive the Baptism of the Holy Spirit. I didn't know if it was really real. It scared me a bit, and I was a skeptic. I wasn't about to buy into any weird or off-the-wall craziness. So I went back to what my friend Donna used to tell me: "Susan, just put whatever you don't understand on the shelf and say 'God, You show me.'" Very good advice. So I decided to ask God to show me if it was real or not.

I spent about a month praying about it, and studying what the Bible had to say about it. After about a month, God began to move on me with His wisdom and guidance. I determined through my own research, that it was indeed real.

I later received the Baptism of the Holy Spirit, worshipping Jesus in a language I had never learned. As I praised Him, I had an awesome manifestation of the presence of Jesus Christ standing right in front of me.

Through the Baptism of the Holy Spirit, a holy door had opened. It was a door introducing me to a fuller aware-ness of the things of God. I had been empowered by the Holy Spirit to live the Christian life and to glorify God by testify-ing to the Gospel of Jesus Christ.

Is It Necessary?

The Baptism of the Holy Spirit is necessary to the Christian life! God doesn't give gifts to His church that are unnecessary. The Baptism of the Holy Spirit gives you POWER to be a witness for Christ. It is a NEW BEGINNING or dimension for the Body of Christ and it enables Christians to be what God has called them to be.

Other Gifts

Besides the Baptism of the Holy Spirit, there are gifts of the Holy Spirit, mentioned in the Bible in 1 Corinthians 12, as well as ministry gifts given to the Church. Jesus is glorified by believers who are filled with the Holy Spirit.

The Body of Christ is a church of POWER. The power of God and the manifested glory of God IN CHRIST is seen through the church functioning the way it did in the Bible. We are seeing it today! Jesus gives us life, and we can have results when we pray—results that can be seen in the believer's life.

Then Peter said to them, "Repent, and let every one of you be bap-

tized in the name of Jesus Christ for the remission of sins, and you shall receive the gift of the Holy spirit. For the gift is to you and to your children, and to all who are afar off, as many as the Lord our God will call." Acts 2:38–39

Authority in Christ

BLESSED BE THE GOD AND FATHER OF OUR LORD
JESUS CHRIST, WHO HAS BLESSED US WITH EVERY
SPIRITUAL BLESSING IN THE HEAVENLY PLACES IN
CHRIST. EPHESIANS 1:3

Since man fell, it became necessary
for a redeemer to come into the
world; likewise a man, but untouched by
the sin that Adam had passed to the
whole human race. That man, who was
God, was Jesus Christ. He came from the
right hand of His Father, taking on the
flesh of man, but untouched by the sin
of man. Through our redemption, Jesus
defeated Satan once and for all.

Jesus Has Given Us Authority

What authority did Jesus give to His followers? First of all we can see through this Scripture in Colossians that Jesus disarmed our enemy once and for all:

Having disarmed principalities and powers, He make a public specta-cle of them, triumphing over them in it. (In the cross.) Colossians 2:15

These Scriptures reveal to the believers in Christ their authority in Christ:

"Behold I give you authority...over all the power of the enemy, and nothing shall by any means hurt you." Luke 10:19

"And these signs will follow those who believe: In My name they will cast out demons..." Mark 16:17

Is Jesus God?

Not only did John say that Jesus was God, the promised savior, but others did. Here is what Peter said of Jesus, as recorded in the Word:

(Jesus) said to them, "But who do you say that I am?" Simon Peter

answered and said, "You are the
Christ, the Son of the living God."
Jesus answered and said to him,
"Blessed are you, Simon Bar-Jonah,
for flesh and blood has not revealed
this to you, but My father who is in
heaven." Matthew 16:15-17

Jesus is recorded as referring to
Himself as the Son of God:

Now Jesus stood before the governor. And the governor asked Him,
saying, "Are You the King of the
Jews?" So Jesus said to him, "It is
as you say." Matthew 27:11

Some people from other religions
have said that Jesus was a great prophet
or that He was *from* God. Great prophets
don't lie; He was who He said He was,
"the Christ the Son of the Living God"
(Matthew 16:16).

John Wrote It
These Scriptures, in the book of John,
confirm the deity of Christ:

In the beginning was the Word,
and the Word was with God, and
the word was God. John 1:1

Jesus was the Word made flesh. He dwelled in our midst. And, as John wrote: The Word, Jesus, was God.

Authority in God's Word

This next spiritual blessing is our authority in Christ. How do we exercise this authority? How can we use this in our everyday lives? There is authority and power in God's Word. The Bible tells us to put on the armor of God:

> *Finally, my brethren, be strong in the Lord and in the power of His might. Put on the whole armor of God, that you may be able to stand against the wiles of the devil. For we do not wrestle against flesh and blood, but against principalities, against powers, against the rulers of the darkness of this age, against spiritual hosts of wickedness in the heavenly places. Therefore take up the whole armor of God, that you may be able to withstand in the evil day, and having done all, to stand. Stand therefore, having girded your waist with truth, having put on the breastplate of righteous-*

*ness, and having shod your feet
with the preparation of the gospel
of peace; above all, taking the
shield of faith with which you will
be able to quench all the fiery
darts of the wicked one. And take
the helmet of salvation, and the
sword of the Spirit, which is the
word of God; praying always with
all prayer and supplication in the
Spirit, being watchful to this end
with all perseverance and supplication for all the saints.*
Ephesians 6:10–18

Our Supernatural Weapons

There is a way to use the authority Christ has given to us. How can we do this?

- **First,** walk in Christ, abiding in Him (John 15:4).

- **Second,** put God and His Word first.

- **Third,** spend time with God and in His Word each day. By doing this, you will stay spiritually built up in Christ. Remember, God's Word is spiritual food (Matthew 1:4). James 1:21 says, "Therefore lay aside all filthiness and

overflow of wickedness, and receive
with meekness the implanted word,
which is able to save your souls." You
are spiritually nourished when you allow
God's Word to become a vital part of
your life. If you don't like to read, get
tapes or CDs to listen to the Bible.

- **Fourth,** pray specifically about the
  problems you or others face in life.
  Follow the prescription for successful
  prayer (on page twenty-seven of this
  book).

- **Fifth,** know in whom you believe and
  rest the whole of your faith on God
  and His promises.

- **Sixth,** realize that your weapons are
  powerful, spiritual weapons.

  *For the weapons of our warfare are
  not carnal but mighty in God for
  pulling down strongholds.*
  2 Corinthians 10:4

Using the Authority

I will always have occasion to take
God at His Word, but quite a number of
years ago, I faced one extremely difficult
time in my life that required strong, and

total faith in God and His promises. There was no other help for me in that situation. I didn't realize it, but I was going to use my authority in Christ. Later I would learn more about this authority in Christ. Here's a brief description of that experience:

I had become a member of a "deliverance" church in the north Georgia mountains. I was sincere, but so young in the things of God that I didn't recognize the Bible error this pastor lived in.

I was looking for a New Testament church where things were done just like they were done in Bible times. It was during the Jesus Movement, and because God was moving so powerfully and miracles abounded, I wanted to attend a church that believed in the miraculous. I was not mature enough in spiritual things to be able to rightly judge my options.

The pastor of the small church I started to attend had plenty of false prophecies and was continually trying to cast the devil out of believers (which is unscriptural). He gave his so-called prophecies, continually telling his members to "repent, and cast that wicked thing out of thy house."

There was no wicked thing in anyone's house. He raved on and on, wreaking havoc on my life and in the lives of the others attending his tiny church.

I began losing my hope and my desire to live. I was too ignorant to recognize the signs that I should get out of there. I didn't know any better, and didn't realize what this man was doing wrong.

I went on four supernatural three-day fasts in one month (no food or water), trying to get answers, and I finally left that church in a weakened, depressed state. I cried out to God Himself. I was about to learn for myself about the authority in God's Word. Isaiah 55:11 says that His Word will never return void. That is the truth. I experienced it for myself. The miracles God proceeded to do in my life as I fasted and prayed, were positive proof of His faithfulness!

No matter who you are and where you live, God can help you when you trust fully in Him and in His promises.

I walked around my home with the sword of the Spirit (Ephesians 6:17), the Word of God, in my mouth. God moved on my behalf, remaining faithful to His promises and His Word to perform it.

God directed me to rest the whole of my faith on His Word and on His promises, and He showed me through Scripture, that He wanted me to be like the Shunammite woman when she needed a miracle and said, "It shall be well," knowing that she was believing in the living God (2 Kings 4:13-34). He also directed me to spend time each day, telling Him my troubles, as He was the Great Physician, able to heal any and all of my troubles. Believe me, I spent time with Him all right...He became my closest friend. I will never be the same.
Seventeen months later, God sent the one person I told Him I could trust to my house.

On September 6, 1976, Pauline got out of her car and came up to my door in the north Georgia mountains: "Susan, God has sent me. Can I come in?"

She went on to tell me about the error of this minister and the difficulties others had experienced because of him.

Authority in Jesus' Name

There was so much I didn't know. If only I had known the authority in the name of Jesus. There is authority in the Word of God, and God still brought a measure of relief to me. Through the steadfastness of the Father's love and through faith in His Word and promises, God rescued me from this situation. I have had to forgive this man.

Nothing's Too Hard For God

Remember that God can take you through any situation. Just trust God and His promises. He is faithful.

Spiritual Healing

BLESSED BE THE GOD AND FATHER OF OUR LORD
JESUS CHRIST, WHO HAS BLESSED US WITH EVERY
SPIRITUAL BLESSING IN THE HEAVENLY PLACES IN
CHRIST. EPHESIANS 1:3

Spiritual health begins at the new birth,
when the life of God, and the divine
seed of God's Word is received into the
spirit of a man or woman. When any person received Jesus Christ as their personal Lord and Savior, a spiritual birth takes
place. The Holy Spirit does His work, making you a supernatural creation in Christ.
The healing that comes to our lives just
because we have accepting Christ into
our lives is the next spiritual blessing.

What Happens Next?

This new birth is a miracle, but the process of transformation and development continues as the newborn Christian continues in the Word of God (by feeding his spirit the spiritual food of God's Word), and by prayer and fellowship with other Spirit-filled believers. A spiritual healing is yours in Christ.

Spiritual deliverance also takes place at the new birth. At the time of the acceptance of Christ, the Lordship of Jesus Christ causes any other power possessing an individual to depart.

Special Cases

Pastoral counseling should be sought for new believers who have left a radical lifestyle. These people may need special help to think correctly. Some of these cases are drug addition, alcoholism, spiritism, criminal behavior, psychological problems, etc. There could also be a need for medical help, in some cases.

A new believer needs to learn how to apply the Word of God to his own life. This can be done by attending a good church, Bible study, and prayer groups.

The new believer will need good
Christian fellowship.

Four Keys to Spiritual Health
Remember these four tips to main-
taining spiritual health in your life:

1. Put God and His Word first. Spend
   time in the Word and in prayer each
   day.

2. Have good Christian friends. You must
   have fun with other Christians. You
   need fellowship. Perhaps you can join
   a small Bible study at your church,
   through which you can make some
   friends. There are good and clean fun
   activities. You need fun in your life.

3. Physical activity. You need some sort
   of physical exercise or outlet. You
   need to attend to physical health–spiritual health and physical health are
   important.

4. Get involved in something at your
   church. You need to get involved. You
   will feel stagnant if there is no outflow
   from your life. Be a blessing.

Giving Spiritual Health to Others

God opened the door for me to minister to some prisoners. These men were living at a center where they were being helped to readjust to society.

I began telling them about the grace of God and healing I had experienced in my own life:

> *God can do anything. He will forgive you of anything. To me, He seems the most powerful where the greatest suffering and needs are. God can heal you spiritually, mentally, emotionally, and physically, and there's NOTHING TOO HARD FOR GOD. God created human life in the first place. If you need the right desires, the desire to serve God, or even to love Him, just tell Jesus about it. It is all through the merits of the redemption that is in Jesus Christ; that is where our riches in Christ and our inheritance proceed from. God can certainly recreate you from the inside out.*

They wanted me to come back and minister to them again. They had heard GOOD NEWS: news about a God whose Son died for them and could even change the WORST case. God could do it! They couldn't change themselves, and maybe some of them didn't even want to be changed. God could make them willing.

"You need a miracle on the INSIDE of you!" I had told the prisoners. They all prayed aloud and asked Jesus Christ to come into their hearts. They had received the greatest miracle. This was their door to spiritual healing.

The developed Christian is full of God's Word, and knows how to apply the Word of God to his or her life and to the lives of others. As the Word of God is built into the spirit of man, he receives healing in his spirit. Then, as the Word of God is built into your spirit, not only does SPIRITUAL HEALING take place, but the provision of Calvary's Cross can also pro-vide mental, emotional, and physical heal-ing. The scriptural proof is here: Matthew 8:17; 1 Peter 2:24; John 14:13 and 15:7; Philippians 4:19; and 3 John 1:2.

What precious and inexpressible power and beauty there is in the Word of God! IT IS LIFE (John 6:63). It is or can be a vital part of your life! It is part of Himself, becoming part of you. The Word of God will have a divine effect upon your life.

Beloved, I pray that you may prosper in all things and be in health, just as your soul prospers.
3 John 1:2

As His divine power has given to us all things that pertain to life and godliness, through the knowledge of Him who called us by glory and virtue, by which have been given to us exceedingly great and precious promises, that through these you may be partakers of the divine nature, having escaped the corruption that is in the world through lust. 2 Peter 1:3,4

Spiritual Growth

BLESSED BE THE GOD AND FATHER OF OUR LORD
JESUS CHRIST, WHO HAS BLESSED US WITH EVERY
SPIRITUAL BLESSING IN THE HEAVENLY PLACES IN
CHRIST. EPHESIANS 1:3

You will grow spiritually and become
spiritually healthy as the Word of God
grows in your life. This spiritual growth is
one of the spiritual blessings that belong
to us as Christians. You will prosper spiritually, but as I have previously stated, the
spiritual blessings in Christ will affect
your natural life as well. God's Word will
lift you up both spiritually and in the
circumstances of your life. As God's Word

is planted in your heart, it will grow and produce fruit like a natural seed. Here are some great Scriptures that talk about God's Word as a seed:

Having been born again, not of corruptible seed but incorruptible, through the Word of God which lives and abides forever.
1 Peter 1:23

"For as the rain comes down, and the snow from heaven, and do not return there, but water the earth, and make it bring forth and bud, that it may give seed to the sower and bread to the eater, so shall my Word be that goes forth from my mouth, it shall not return to Me void, but it shall accomplish what I please, and it shall prosper in the thing for which I sent it."
Isaiah 55:10,11

How Can I Grow?
When you hear the Word through anointed teaching or preaching and through meditation in the Word of God, it is going to nourish your spirit and you will grow spiritually (Matthew 4:4, James 1:21).

"It is the Spirit who gives life; the flesh profits nothing. The words that I speak to you are spirit, and they are life." John 6:63

The Word of God is an undamage-able, incorruptible seed. It lives...it abides (remains; stays) forever:

...Having been born again, not of corruptible seed but incorruptible, through the word of God which lives and abides forever, 1 Peter 2:23

There is supernatural power within the Word of God. During the Jesus Movement, kids who had been on drugs began to read the Bible. Surprisingly, their minds began to heal:

For this reason we also thank God without ceasing, because when you received the word of God which you heard from us, you welcomed it not as the word of men, but as it is in truth, the word of God, which also effectively works in you who believe. 1 Thessalonians 2:13

Lay aside all filthiness and over-flow of wickedness, and receive

67

with meekness the implanted
word, which is able to save your
souls. James 1:21

God Uses People

God uses people to speak His Word in anointed preaching, teaching, etc., and when they speak the Word, it produces a Holy Spirit fruit (not to be confused with the fruit of the spirit), outward fruit in their everyday circumstances.

It is the spirit that quickeneth; the
flesh profiteth nothing: the words
that I speak unto you, they are
spirit, and they are life. John 6:63

In John 6:63, Jesus said that His words *are* spirit and life. The word "life" in the Greek is *zoe.* What does that mean?

The *Vine's Expository Dictionary of New Testament Words* says:

Life, as a noun, 2222, zoe:
(Eng., "zoo," "zoology") is used in the NT "of life as a principle, life in the absolute sense, life as God has it, that which the Father has in

Himself, and which He gave to the Incarnate Son to have in Himself, John 5:26, and which the Son manifested in the world, 1 John 1:2. From this life man has become alienated in consequence of the fall, Eph. 4:18, and of this life men become partakers through faith in the Lord Jesus Christ, John 3:15, who becomes its Author to all such as trust in Him, Acts 3:15, and who is therefore said to be 'the life' of the believer, Colossians 3:4, for the life that He gives He maintains, John 6:35,63.

Life as a verb, 2227, zoopoieo: "to make alive, cause to live, quicken (from zoe, "life," and poieo, "to make") is used as follows in John 6:63: of the impartation of spiritual life, and the communi-cation of spiritual sustenance gen-erally, John 6:63; 2 Cor. 3:6; Gal. 3:21." * (* From Notes on Galatians, by Hogg and Vine, pp. 154,155.)

The Word and the Spirit

The Holy Spirit will cause the Word of God that has been planted in your spirit to produce a godly fruit. Proverbs 4 contains good tips for spiritual growth:

> *My son, give attention to my words; Incline your ear to my sayings. Do not let them depart from your eyes; Keep them in the midst of your heart; For they are life to those who find them, And health to all their flesh. Keep your heart with all diligence, For out of it spring the issues of life. Put away from you a deceitful mouth, And put perverse lips far from you. Let your eyes look straight ahead, And your eyelids look right before you. Ponder the path of your feet, And let all your ways be established. Do not turn to the right or the left; Remove your foot from evil.*
> Proverbs 4:20-27

That says it all. Do those things, and you will grow.

A Renewed Mind

You can have a mind renewed by the Word of God. To enjoy scriptural thoughts, thoughts that are holy and sound, is spiritual prosperity. The Bible tells us what the fruit is: "But the fruit of the Spirit is love, joy, peace, longsuffering, kindness, goodness, faithfulness, gentleness, self-control. Against such there is no law" (Gal. 5:22,23). God is limitless in what He can do in your life:

Now unto Him who is able to do exceedingly abundantly above all that we ask or think, according to the power that works in us.
Ephesians 3:20

Your Spiritual Weapon

If you've ever felt discouraged or depressed, the enemy will always tell you it's God's fault, or that God doesn't care. Do what Jesus did. Take the Word of God and Jesus' name as a weapon, submit to God, resist the devil, and he will flee (James 4:7).

For we do not wrestle against flesh and blood, but against principali-

71

ties, against powers, against the
rulers of the darkness of this age,
against spiritual hosts of wicked-
ness in the heavenly places.
Ephesians 6:12

In this life we aren't playing games.
There is a very real battle going on. The
Word of God is the choice weapon for
the spiritual realm. It is not a natural
weapon but a supernatural weapon.
   In the book of Ephesians, Paul
teaches the body of Christ about their
armor:

And take the helmet of salvation,
and the sword of the spirit which
is the word of God; praying always
with all prayer and supplication in
the Spirit, being watchful to this
end with all perseverance and sup-
plication for all the saints...
Ephesians 6:17–18

Note that it says, "praying always."

For the Word of God is living and
powerful, and sharper than any
two-edged sword, piercing even to
the division of soul and spirit, and
of joints and marrow, and is a dis-

72

*cerner of the thoughts and intents
of the heart.* Hebrews 4:12

Not A Game

You can become a master swordsman. Learning to apply and use the Word
of God properly is like the difference
between children playing sword fights
and a master swordsman who, after
much training, has developed his skill.
He is a master at what he does. The mus-
cles he uses have become developed
and strong. He has learned, through
experience, what moves to make and
when. He has become quick, and when
he strikes with the sword, he hits his tar-
get forcefully. It didn't come overnight,
but now, after much training he has
become a MASTER SWORDSMAN.

We need to become master swords-
men with the Word of God. Jesus replied
with Scripture to temptation (Matthew 4).
The Word of God coming out of His
mouth was His sword.

The Word of God is the sword of the
Spirit. You can do what Jesus did, but
don't forget this vital part of the scripture:
"Praying always with all prayer and supplication in the Spirit" (Ephesians 6:17,18).

Supernatural Power

There is supernatural power in the Word of God. It is spiritual food, and it is the sword of the Spirit. The enemy must flee in the name of Jesus, and God's Word is a weapon. Notice what the Bible says Jesus did for us: "Having disarmed principalities and powers, He made a public spectacle of them, triumphing them in it" (Colossians 2:15).

Satan is the *defeated* enemy. Jesus has already defeated him for you through the redemptive work of the Cross of Calvary. Satan has no legal right in the Christian's life. This really comes alive for us through prayer and through learning how to obtain God's promises for our own lives.

For the weapons of our warfare are not carnal, but mighty in God to the pulling down of strongholds...
2 Corinthians 10:4

Don't forget that when the Bible tells us to resist the enemy of our lives, He also says, "Resist him steadfast in the faith" (1 Peter 5:9).

Not: "Name It, Claim It"

The Word of God is a sword against the enemy and an effectual weapon. But also remember that the promises of God are true. You can go to the Father, in Jesus' name and in prayer, and claim the promises of God (Philippians 4:6,7). Hold on a minute. This is not "name it, claim it." No! This is resting the whole of our trust in God and His promises. This is claiming, or laying hold of this, for "me" personally.

> *For all the promises of God in Him*
> *are Yes, and in Him Amen, to the*
> *glory of God through us.*
> 1 Corinthians 1:20

Note that the verse says ALL of the promises are "yes, and in Him Amen." The Lord will move on your behalf as you trust Him and His Word. There is tremendous limitless power in God. Think about it. But remember to be vigilant, "that you do not become sluggish, but imitate those who through faith and patience inherit the promises." (Hebrews 6:12)

Receiving These Blessings

BLESSED BE THE GOD AND FATHER OF OUR LORD
JESUS CHRIST, WHO HAS BLESSED US WITH EVERY
SPIRITUAL BLESSING IN THE HEAVENLY PLACES IN
CHRIST. EPHESIANS 1:3

You can receive all of these great spiritual blessings in your life. Would you
like to? If you have not experienced the
life and love of God in Jesus Christ, or if
you never knew that there was life for
you through the redemptive word of
Jesus Christ when He shed His blood,
dying for you on the cross and then rising
again from the dead, repeat this prayer:

Jesus, forgive me of all my sins. I believe that You died on the cross for my sins and rose again from the dead. Come inside of my heart, into the very depths of my being through Your Holy Spirit, right now. I make You the Lord and Savior of my life. Take control of my life, and make me into the person you want me to be. Amen. John, 3:16; Romans 10:9,10

What Next?

Here is what you do next:

- Let God begin to change and mold your life. It will be obvious.

- Let Him reveal the rich treasures that are yours because of what His Son Jesus has already done for you on the Cross.

- Have a "quiet time" with God each day, even if it's only a few minutes to begin with. In this time, you will talk to Him and tell Him what's going on in your life. You can share everything with Him, even though He knows it anyway. Although you can talk to God all day, this is a good time to tell Him

78

your requests for your life, the lives of others, and anything you want to pray for in the world. I'm convinced that God loves this. I found that when I shared things with Him, even without asking, He would do things for me in these areas. Why? Well, He really is alive. He cares for and loves you more than you can comprehend. Your relationship with Him will grow.

- Read the Bible. Through the Word, your spirit will be fed and healed, and you will grow spiritually.

- Get involved with a worshiping, prayer-believing, power-of-God-believing church. Hebrews 10:25 says, "Not forsaking the assembling of ourselves together, as is the manner of some, but exhorting one another, and so much the more as you see the day approaching."

Manifested Blessings

There is no need to feel overwhelmed. Just begin where you are. You will begin to experience these blessings in your own life. The amount of time you spend in your quiet time or prayer time will change depending on God's call for your life. Do not feel condemnation about it. Just enjoy your relationship with God.

As you go to church and Bible studies, and listen to anointed teaching and preaching, God's Word will heal your life spiritually, mentally, emotionally, and physically, according to His will.

It doesn't matter how great your need. He is limitless in His ability to work in your life. Don't doubt it for a minute. No matter what the need, God is greater! His Word is greater, and there is nothing too hard for God (Jeremiah 32:27). Let God do a mighty work in you by the power of His Holy Spirit and through His Word. Remember that His Word is working on the inside of you:

> *For this reason we also thank God*
> *without ceasing, because when you*
> *received the Word of God which*
> *you heard from us, you welcomed*
> *it not as the word of men, but as it*
> *is in truth, the Word of God, which*
> *also effectively works in you who*
> *believe.* 1Thessalonians 2:13

God has made provision for all of

your needs through the redemptive work of the cross. Trust in God. Trust in the power in the shed blood of the Lord Jesus Christ, in the power of the Holy Spirit, and in the power of the Word of God.

God is Who He says He is, and He can do what His Word says He can do. Ephesians 1:3 tells us that we have been given spiritual blessings in and through the Lord Jesus Christ! HAVE BEEN GIVEN THEM...past tense. These spiritual blessings in heavenly places in Christ belong to you. They belong to us all.

What hope there is in salvation by the blood of Jesus Christ, the Promised One, the Savior, and just think: He can become our own personal Lord! God is no respecter of persons. His grace is great enough to forgive you, whatever the sin. His love and mercy extend to all. So too, is His power to save us and to forgive us. He is far greater than any of us can imagine. HE LIVES.

Scriptures for Meditation

BLESSED BE THE GOD AND FATHER OF OUR LORD
JESUS CHRIST, WHO HAS BLESSED US WITH EVERY
SPIRITUAL BLESSING IN THE HEAVENLY PLACES IN
CHRIST. EPHESIANS 1:3

I have included some of my favorite
Scriptures in this last chapter. I have
found great comfort in the Bible.
Remember that as you hear or read the
Word of God, and as you meditate on it,
you will grow spiritually.

During an outpouring of the Holy
Spirit several years ago, there was a story
going around about three teenagers who
were all on LSD. They had the same trip
at the same time on the side of a hill.

They envisioned the night sky full of stars. All of a sudden, they saw large hands roll up the sky like a scroll and the stars flee away. A girl in the group was a preacher's daughter. She remembered that in the book of Revelation there was a Scripture that told of something like that.

Then the sky receded as a scroll when it is rolled up, and every mountain and island was moved out of its place. Revelation 6:14

They ran to a church to give their lives to Christ. The next thing that happened is even better. Many kids whose minds had been damaged through the use of drugs, found that by reading the Bible their minds were healed.

Enjoy these Scriptures. I pray that each one will be built into you and that it will produce a great harvest of fruit in your lives.

If you abide in Me, and My words abide in you, you will ask what you desire, and it shall be done for you. John 15:7

This Book of the Law shall not depart from your mouth, but you shall meditate in it day and night, that you may observe to do according to all that is written in it. For then you will make your way prosperous, and then you will have good success. Joshua 1:8

For this reason we also thank God without ceasing, because when you received the word of God which you heard from us, you welcomed it NOT as the word of men, but as it is in truth, the word of God, which also effectually works in you who believe. I Thessalonians 2:13

"It is the Spirit who gives life; the flesh profits nothing. the words that I speak to you are spirit, and they are life." John 6:63

"So shall My Word be that goes forth from My mouth; it shall not return to Me void, but it shall accomplish what I please, and it shall prosper in the thing for which I sent it." Isaiah 55:11

...As His divine power has given to us all things that pertain to life and godliness, through the knowledge of Him who called us by glory and virtue, by which have been given to us exceeding great and precious promises, that through these you may be partakers of the divine nature... 2 Peter 1:3,4

And what is the exceeding greatness of His power toward us who believe, according to the working of His mighty power which He worked in Christ when He raised Him from the dead... Ephesians 1:19,20

For we are His workmanship, created in Christ Jesus for good works, which God prepared beforehand that we should walk in them. Ephesians 2:10

In Time of Trouble

He who has begun a good work in you will complete it until the day of Jesus Christ. Philippians 1:6

*And the Lord will deliver me from
every evil work and preserve me
for His heavenly kingdom. To Him
be glory forever and ever. Amen!* 2
Timothy 4:18

For Protection

*No evil shall befall you, nor shall
any plague come near your
dwelling; For He shall give His
angels charge over you, to keep
you in all your ways.*
Psalms 91:10,11

Promises for Answered Prayer

*Be anxious for nothing, but in
everything by prayer and supplication, with thanksgiving, let your
requests be made known to God
and the peace of God, which sur-
passes all understanding, will guard
your hearts and minds through
Christ Jesus.* Philippians 4:6-7

*And whatever you ask in My name,
that I will do, that the Father may be
glorified in the son. If you ask anything in My name, I will do it.*
John 14:13–14

And in that day you will ask Me nothing. Most assuredly, I say to you, whatever you ask the Father in My name He will give you. Until now you have asked nothing in My name. Ask, and you will receive, that your joy may be full. John 16:23–24

For all the promises of God in Him are Yes, and in Him Amen, to the glory of God through us. 2 Corinthians 1:20

Now unto Him who is able to do exceedingly abundantly above all that we ask or think, according to the power that works in us, to Him be glory in the church by Christ Jesus to all generations, forever and ever. Amen. Ephesians 3:20–21

And my God shall supply all your need according to His riches in glory by Christ Jesus. Philippians 4:19

Now this is the confidence that we have in Him, that if we ask anything according to His will, He hears us. And if we know He hears

*us, whatever we ask, we know that
we have the petitions that we have
asked of Him.* 1 John 5:14–15

*Therefore humble yourselves under
the mighty hand of God, that He
may exalt you in due time, casting
all your care upon Him, for He cares
for you.* 1 Peter 5:6-7

JESUS' WORDS

*"And when you pray, you shall not
be like the hypocrites. For they
love to pray standing in the syna-
gogues and on the corners of the
streets, that they may be seen by
men. Assuredly, I say to you, they
have their reward. But you, when
you pray, go into your room, and
when you have shut your door,
pray to your Father who is in the
secret place; and your Father who
sees in secret will reward you
openly. And when you pray, do not
use vain repetitions as the hea-
then do. For they think that they
will be heard for their many words.
Therefore do not be like them. For*

your Father knows the things you have need of before you ask Him. In this manner, therefore, pray:

Our Father in heaven, hallowed be Your name. Your kingdom come. Your will be done on earth as it is in heaven. Give us this day our daily bread. And forgive us our debts, as we forgive our debtors. And do not lead us into temptation, but deliver us from the evil one. For Yours is the kingdom and the power and the glory forever. Amen. For if you forgive men their trespasses, your heavenly Father will also forgive you. But if you do not forgive men their trespasses, neither will your Father forgive your trespasses."
Matthew 6:5–15

CHAPTER TWELVE

Spiritual Reflection

R eflect now on this blessing. Write
down your thoughts. Think about
how thankful you are for this blessing.
God has given you life!

_____

_____

_____

_____

_____

www.ingramcontent.com/pod-product-compliance
Lightning Source LLC
Chambersburg PA
CBHW071015040426
42443CB00007B/792